Stuart Morris was born on Portland, and his roots on the Island go back many generations. His interest in Portland's history was fostered by the discovery of his family's involvement with quarrying, the Breakwater, fishing and even smuggling. For twelve years he represented Portland on the Dorset County Council, and was an ardent campaigner for the local environment. From 1991 he was the Highways Agency Manager for the local Borough Council, retiring in 2000. He was a founder member of the Portland Field Research Group and the Isle of Portland Heritage Trust, and he is a patron of the Royal Manor Workshops. As well as photography, Stuart's interests include technology, music and the arts. He is married with three grown-up children and five grandchildren. He is the author of *Portland, An Illustrated History* (1985), *Portland Camera* (1990), *Discover Dorset, Portland* (1998), *Portland, A Portrait in Colour* (2002), and other local books.

Following pages
1. Looking down on Fortune's Well before the Great War.
Shops lined both sides of this long narrow street from end-to-end; shoppers could buy everything they needed within walking distance. Upper right was St Johns School of 1857 (see Fortune's Well chapter). The modern photograph shows the gaps in the street frontage left by Second World War bomb damage, but 20th-century traffic contributed to the demise of Fortune's Well as the Island's shopping centre. Between the old and the new pictures, the Mere (top) has changed from natural salt water shallows to a fuel tank farm, then a major naval helicopter base, and now in 2006 is developing as the country's leading sports sailing complex.

PORTLAND
THEN & NOW

Stuart Morris

THE DOVECOTE PRESS

2. Queen Victoria was still Lady of the Royal Manor when this trio of Easton girls stood before the camera. The old thatched cottage behind them has long gone, but the stones of the house next door remain as they were laid some 200 years before.

First published in 2006
by The Dovecote Press Ltd
Stanbridge, Wimborne Minster, Dorset BH21 4JD

ISBN 1 904349 48 X

Designed by The Dovecote Press Ltd
Printed and bound in Singapore

A CIP catalogue record for this book is available
from the British Library

Contents

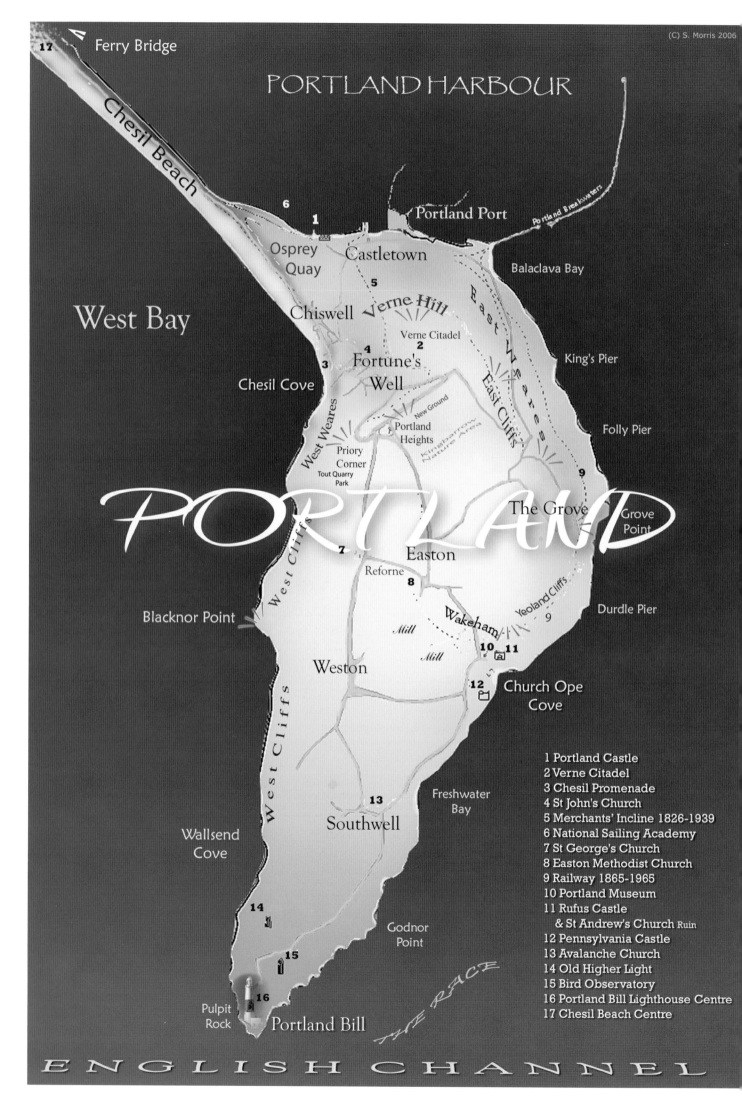

17 Ferry Bridge

PORTLAND HARBOUR

Chesil Beach

6 **1**

Portland Port

Portland Breakwaters

Osprey Quay

Castletown

Balaclava Bay

West Bay

Chiswell

5 Verne Hill

East Weares

Verne Citadel

2

King's Pier

4 Fortune's

3 Well

Chesil Cove

East Cliffs

New Ground

West Weares

Portland Heights

Folly Pier

Priory Corner

Kingbarrow Nature Area

Tout Quarry Park

9

PORTLAND

The Grove

Grove Point

7

Easton

Reforne

8

Yeoland Cliffs

West Cliffs

Blacknor Point

Wakeham

9

Durdle Pier

Mill

10 **11**

Weston

Mill

12 Church Ope Cove

1 Portland Castle
2 Verne Citadel
3 Chesil Promenade
4 St John's Church
5 Merchants' Incline 1826-1939
6 National Sailing Academy
7 St George's Church
8 Easton Methodist Church
9 Railway 1865-1965
10 Portland Museum
11 Rufus Castle
   & St Andrew's Church Ruin
12 Pennsylvania Castle
13 Avalanche Church
14 Old Higher Light
15 Bird Observatory
16 Portland Bill Lighthouse Centre
17 Chesil Beach Centre

West Cliffs

Freshwater Bay

13

Southwell

Wallsend Cove

14

Godnor Point

15

THE RACE

Pulpit Rock

16

Portland Bill

ENGLISH CHANNEL

Introduction

Portland had a young and vibrant population in the late Victorian/Edwardian period. Everyone seemed eager to keep in touch with friends and relations by the quickest means possible. Telephones were still a rarity but the postal service was excellent, often with 'same day' local deliveries. The science of photography was maturing, enabling day-to-day images to be mass-produced in the form of picture postcards. Enterprising individuals set up photographic studios on the Island, usually associated with chemists and picture framing businesses. These included John S. Coombe, Frederick W. George (later King), and William Thompson. Visiting photographers included Edwin Seward of Weymouth, and the famous Francis Frith.

Those pioneers produced a remarkable record of Island life and scenes that were destined to change in ways they could never imagine. Despite their heavy cameras and the complex developing processes, the pictures they produced were often technically brilliant. Anyone with half an eye for photography will recognise how carefully composed were many of the old photographs; how the photographer had waited for the optimum lighting conditions, and posed passers-by to add charming life to static street scenes. Many Victorian photographs display a sharpness and depth of quality that can hardly be surpassed even today.

The brief Edwardian period, 1901 to 1910, was the golden age of the picture postcard, hence the number of photographs from that period in this book. It was a time of much historic advancement on Portland. That remarkable decade saw the railway arriving at Easton, the new lighthouse, and the final stages of the Breakwaters. The Royal Naval Hospital (now Portland Hospital) arose at Castletown; the first of the huge oil tanks appeared on the Mere behind Chesil Beach, and new quays and jetties were constructed on the harbour-side. The quarries were booming. With prosperity came an explosion of leisure pursuits, exemplified by the glorious Easton and Victoria Gardens, and Underhill's Cadets' Recreation Ground. Religion was still important and around this same short period two large Wesleyan churches were built, at Fortune's Well and Easton.

Many of Portland's surviving historic buildings look much as they did in the old photographs. The greatest physical change has been in the Island's landscape. In the early 20th-century most of Tophill was still largely pastoral, with the villages of

3. Ancient cottages nestle on the back of the beach in the historic village of Chiswell. Some of the fishermen's houses have gone, but others have been carefully restored. The promenade, built between 1958 and 1965 to protect the coast, is now a superb amenity.

Wakeham, Weston and Southwell nestling among coast-to-coast fields. The quarries had not yet gorged their way across these ancient farmlands, and the sprawling late 20th-century housing estates were far into the future. The sequence of views of Underhill shows how much green land has been lost there.

It is unfair to compare old black and white views with new colour ones. Earlier times of course were just as colourful as now, and for the Edwardians it was even more so. Theirs was a time of flamboyant dresses and beautiful hats, smart boaters, picnic teas and carnivals. The grass was as green and the sky as blue - if only colour photography had been available then! Because we can only see the past in monochrome, both 'Then' and 'Now' photographs in this volume are in black and white. I hope that when browsing through this book, seeking out the differences which time has imposed upon our island, you will find the changes as intriguing as I have.

The old photographs are windows through which

we can glimpse the characters of long ago, and the places that were familiar to them. The modern pictures show those same places – the same ground on which those earlier Portlanders walked, worked and played. Much has changed, and I have found matching new with the old an enjoyable challenge. For the majority of the new photos I have stood on the same spot on which those earlier photographers set up their tripods, although in a few cases this was physically impossible. Images taken through fixed lenses onto glass plates have different characteristics and perspectives than those from modern cameras. In many cases I have tried to digitally adjust the 'Now' images to compensate for this.

The photographs in this book span the whole of the 20th century and beyond. Such has been the pace of change that some of the 'Then' pictures I took myself! To see what has happened for instance at Ferry Bridge, Chesil Cove and Priory Corner in the past 50 years can be just as interesting as looking further back.

I pay tribute to the numerous friends and acquaintances who have helped me over many years to build up my collection, from which these old images are taken. They have shared my desire to make this historic material available to everyone.

The 'Now' pictures are but a snapshot in the Island's timeline, but if nothing else I would like to think they provide a portrait of Portland in the early 21st century that accurately reflects both its historic

4. Local people crowd around the scene of *Mr Midshipman Easy* being filmed on West Cliff in 1935. Standing by the horse is 16-year-old Hughie Green, later of TV quiz fame. The actress Margaret Lockwood also starred in this thriller. The massive rock structures were built in the early 19th century to support a rail tramway bridge for tipping quarry overburden over the cliff.

character and the optimism of its present. I only hope that a *Portland, Then and Now* 100 years hence will show that, whatever the future changes, the best of this unique Island remains intact.

Stuart Morris
Portland, September 2006

Ferry Bridge

5. The opening of the first Ferry Bridge in 1839 was a momentous milestone in Portland's history. The original timber structure was replaced by an iron bridge in 1895. Designed by Sir John Coode in the age of the horse and cart, this bridge carried every vehicle moving on and off the Island for 90 years. It was finally replaced in 1985 by a sleek new stone-faced bridge further to the south, off to the left. The Portland/Weymouth boundary remains across the centre of Smallmouth waters (foreground). The Ferry Bridge pub (centre) stands on the site of the ancient ferryman's house.

Portland Harbour

6. The great Breakwaters forming Portland Harbour were constructed in 2 phases between 1848 and 1906. For more than 100 years, Portlanders and visitors enjoyed a magnificent spectacle whenever the Fleet was in. In 1998 the Coaling Pier, seen here just after its 1903-6 extension, was transformed into a major commercial undersea cable facility. The Royal Navy formally departed from Portland in 1995 auguring great changes for the area.

7. The first major development after the Second World War was the building of a new deepwater jetty; Queen's (or 'Q') Pier. Contractor A.E. Farr drove 500 22m long piles into the seabed from a giant mobile gantry. They also reclaimed a large area to extend the working foreshore. Behind are some of the Phoenix units that formed part of the wartime Mulberry Harbour, towed back here from the French coast after being used to form a sheltered harbour following the Normandy landings in 1944. Through the next 45 years, Portland played host to countless ships of the NATO navies. Even today, two of the 60 metre long Phoenix units remain to give shelter to vessels moored alongside Q-Pier.

Morris Collection

8. By the 1890s when this old picture was taken Castletown's Stone Pier had a dual purpose: Here, stone brought down via the Merchants' Incline was loaded onto vessels, while paddle steamers from Weymouth landed increasing numbers of visitors. In the 1960s, the pier was dominated by huge aggregate-handling plant, but today it is a scene of yachts and pleasure craft.

9. The East Weares was for hundreds of years the scene of frenetic activity with the stone from cliff-edge quarries carted down to several barge-loading piers on the shore. The RN Rifle Range (lower centre) dates from 1903, and the buildings (centre) – demolished in 2005 – were the offices, training school, laboratories and mess of Portland's secret Admiralty research establishment, HMS *Osprey*. The drilling rig, centre in this 2006 view, is delving an incredible two kilometres below seabed level for the prospect of storing natural gas. The rifle range along with two sports pitches are no more. The area is a supremely rich natural environment.

10. The Victorians built Folly Pier Waterworks to serve the Grove convict prison. Both fresh rainwater and seawater were stored in separate reservoirs before being pumped up to the cliff-top jail. Coal for the pump boiler was landed from ketches or schooners at the nearby ancient Folly Pier and was conveyed by horse and cart (right). Nature has now nearly reclaimed her ground in East Weares.

Castletown & the Mere

11. Castletown developed along with the Navy through the late 19th century. Its range of businesses from ships chandlery, foreign exchange facility, bespoke naval tailors, a post office and, of course, pubs, were well placed along the narrow waterfront – the main way into the naval port. With the departure of the Navy, the nature of the area changed markedly reflecting the sea change in Portland Harbour. Professional and recreational diving businesses are among the many new enterprises that have sprung up. The waters around Portland offer first class diving opportunities. The old Customs house (left) is now a private house.

12. Castletown's grand Victorian pubs have been progressively refurbished, but there is now no sign of the old Castle Hotel or of the tiny barber's shop tucked onto its side. The latter was much lower than the surrounding ground and was probably on the original beach level at this point.

Designed to impress, the Royal Breakwater and Portland Roads hotels (right) flaunt the strikingly bold architecture of their era.

13. Among the Score family's businesses around 1920 were this large ship chandlery and bakery at the entrance to Castletown Pier. Next door was the Salvation Army Sailors Home (later the Red Shield Hostel) which was established just before the First World War. The railway lines carried trucks from the Merchants Incline to the Stone Pier. The anchor is a nautical feature in Castletown's recently enhanced street.

14. Iron railings separate the visiting crowds disembarking from Cosens' paddle steamer *Premier* from the working area of Castletown's Stone Pier. Some of these elegant Edwardian ladies are tempted by the penny-in-the-slot machine. The first proper pier in this area was built in 1825 as the destination for stone brought down by the Merchants Railway.

The pier's west side is now the working part, for shellfish processing, whilst the 'fun' section – off to the right – is now filled with recreational sailing craft.

15. The horses have just been unhitched from the wagon carrying this huge stone block. The truck is being prepared for descent of the Merchants Incline. Supervisor William Mellish (left) is keeping a careful eye on the potentially dangerous operation. The steel ropes rolled over the recessed wheels and the speed of descent was controlled by a large brake drum in the building behind. The other end of the cable was hitched to empty trucks, which were thus drawn up at the same time.

Remnants of the railway can still be seen among the grass. The arch, which carries the zigzag road to the Verne, replaced the old steel Red Bridge in 1983.

16. A single truck begins its descent of the Merchants Incline to Castletown in about 1905. The signal was installed after a bridge carrying the public railway to Easton obscured the line of sight for the operators. The grassland of Verne Hill was still close-cropped by grazing as it had been for time immemorial. The entire Merchants Railway including the incline is now a public footpath. From here are splendid panoramic views over Chesil B each and West Bay.

17. The tools and equipment for the delicate operation of lowering the stone down the extremely steep incline are clearly shown in this picture. The stresses and wear and tear on the ropes, chains, rails and braking mechanism were closely monitored, and diligently recorded by the supervisor. The Merchants Railway closed in 1939 on the outbreak of the Second World War. The old railway now provides a very useful continuous walk from Portland Heights to Castletown. Fortunately its route was preserved when land each side of the incline was built upon in the late 20th century.

18. (*Above top*) To the lee of Chesil Beach was the ancient Mere, separated from Portland Harbour by a shingle bank called Coneygar. Tidal water flowed through a narrow gap – 'The Gut' – that historically gave access to the shallow waters; a harbour for small boats possibly since Roman times. The first of the naval oil tanks was built in 1907. The long pier supported a pumpline for seabed sand, used for reclamation, augmented by pebbles from Chesil Beach! Incredibly most of the large buildings in the first picture were built within just 6 years before 1910.

(*Above*) The second view shows the helicopter base in 1963. The Verne Common hillside (foreground) was by then covered with houses. 'RN Helicopter Station, Portland' was formally commissioned on the 24th April 1959. Anti-submarine detection operations by '737' and later squadrons grew rapidly. Twelve more acres (5 ha) of land were reclaimed from the harbour in 1971-74. All that is now history; here now is the Weymouth and Portland National Sailing Academy, formally opened by the Princess Royal in 2005.

(*Opposite page top*) 1996; the enlarged airfield, helicopter hangars and repair buildings, and (right) huge 1987 naval accommodation blocks – the Hardy Site. The largest military helicopter base in Europe finally closed in 1999, completing the demise of *HMS Osprey* and all naval and Admiralty facilities on Portland.

(*Opposite page bottom*) Transformation: The old Mere is now *Osprey Quay*, and the site of the Olympic standard Weymouth & Portland National Sailing Academy. The last of the 100 year-old oil tanks are going, but the busy Search and Rescue helicopter makes good use of the remaining airstrip. A new 600-berth marina is also to be built here, whose plans include restaurants, chandlery, yacht brokerage and marine engineers.

19. By 1976 some of the naval oil tanks had dominated the approach to Portland for 70 years. The chequered building generated steam for heating buildings within the naval base, taken there by insulated pipelines. The stone wall alongside the beach road was built to prevent horses shying from trains on the track that ran close behind it. The wall was destroyed in catastrophic sea flooding in 1978 and 1979, and later the road was raised above flood level. The new picture shows the outlet from a huge culvert buried within the beach, which intercepts floodwater. Maritime factory units stand in the place of the cylindrical fuel tanks, and behind them is a luxury yacht manufacturer.

20. Most of this inter-war scene from Chesil Beach has changed beyond recognition. The Verne Common hillside was still grassland, where Portlanders' had traditional rights to graze their sheep and cattle. It was also a vast free playground for generations of children. The chimney, lower left was on F.J. Barnes' stone masonry works; two traction engine loads a day arrived here from the quarries. Next to it is the railway goods station, and behind is the gas works. The recent view shows the extent of the housing estate built on the Verne Common in the 1950s. The entire foreground industrial complex has vanished.

21. 1956; another view from the beach. Railway trucks stand on the approach to the Portland goods station, Victoria Square. The line to Easton curves around towards Castletown and passes under Castle Road near the pair of oil tanks. Portland Castle can be seen upper left. From the same standpoint in 2006 a wide green sward has been formed. This is designed to release any sea floodwater from Chiswell, a function that the old tidal Mere used to perform naturally. The large dark buildings in the distance were naval accommodation blocks built in 1987. Twenty years later, these are being converted into brighter civilian apartments.

Chiswell

22. A charming street scene at the south end of Chiswell village circa 1898. Behind the children is Tom Flew's grocery and bakery, which produced some of the best traditional Portland dough cake. There are five shops in this small corner alone. Note the survival of the oriel window on the right.

23. The stones of Chiswell's old Crown Inn could tell many stories. In 1823 the first Sunday school treat was held in this 18th-century hostelry, with beef and plum pudding served. Before being marched back up to Fortune's Well, the children were each given an orange – a very rare fruit in those days.

The steep road winding around the Crown Inn was far too narrow to accommodate 20th-century traffic, so in 1962 the old pub was demolished to make way for a one-way system.

24. Victorian and Edwardian Portlanders enjoyed nothing more than a good rousing procession. If no bands were available, they would make up for it by singing. Smiles and laughter shows in the faces of these Fortune's Well Primitive Methodist members, although some were heading straight for the horse droppings!

The modern scene of the same part of Chiswell shows how differently the old streets are used in the 21st century.

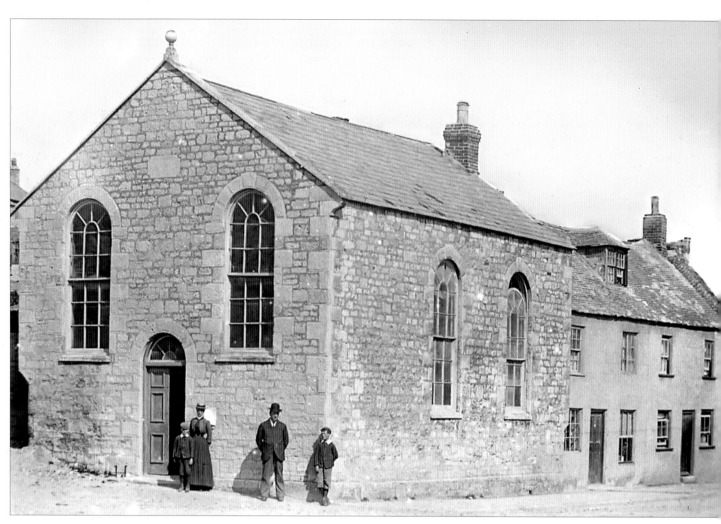

25. The 19th century saw an astonishing amount of chapel building on Portland: Islanders warmed to the informality of the Methodist movement, which also helped to control the 'drunken influences' of soldiers and sailors based here. This early Victorian chapel at Chiswell gave moral guidance to generations of villagers into the 20th century. It was converted into flats in the 1970s.

26. A quiet sunny morning in the 'shopping centre' of old Chiswell village. You could buy almost anything in the tiny shops along this wide street in the 1920s. There were greengrocers, a barber, sweet shops, a butcher, a cobbler, dairy shops, newsagent, and of course – being so close to the beach – fishmongers. Some of the old cottages and all the shops have now gone, but with careful restoration, much remains of historic Chiswell to keep its unique character alive.

27. All friends together on the Island's 'Children's Day' parades, still going strong in the late 1920s. No televisions or computer screens then to keep youngsters closeted in their bedrooms. The large chapel (left) is the United Reformed Church, erected in 1858. In the centre is one of Underhill's finest buildings, being restored in 2006. Work on this possibly 400-year-old house has revealed long-hidden features, including several large rooms below present ground level.

28. Early photographers could see the inherent charm in these old cottages in Brandy Row. Such thatched buildings were to be found in every village on Portland. Although exposed to storm lashing it was not sea flooding which destroyed the last of these; it was the strident policy of the Portland Council between the wars, which decreed that old buildings should not be modernised but demolished. Architectural historian Eric Ricketts said that restoration of this original street scene would make it 'as attractive as Dorset's Milton Abbas'. Maybe one day . . .

The top photograph on the opposite page shows the cottages in about 1895, whilst the larger photograph dates to only a few years later. The modern photograph above was taken in the spring of 2006.

29. The exceptionally wide highway at the north end of Chiswell. The late 19th century West Bay Terrace was later extended into the walled enclosure called Mongers Ground (left). Next to the Terminus Hotel (right) was the Lord Clyde Inn, named after a rather unlucky warship that frequented Portland Harbour. The pub suffered bomb damage in the Second World War and never reopened. The solitary gas light on the right was lit by a lamplighter, whose round extended from Priory Corner to Castletown. He carried a long pole with a hook on one end and a paraffin soaked rag on the other. On winter evenings children gathered in the pool of light under the lamps to play marbles or spinning tops. In the daytime there was plenty of space to play safely in the road.

30. This turn-of-the-century street scene in Chiswell speaks for itself. The children were clearly happy to have been rounded up for the photographer, who would have taken several minutes to prepare his camera. Externally, many of the houses on the right in West Bay Terrace remain largely unchanged. The most obvious difference between the two photographs is the disappearance of the railway station, the neat twin-gabled building in the background.

31. Victoria Square was designed as an entity in the 1860s to coincide with the arrival of the railway. The southwest corner was marked by the Terminus Hotel (the railway terminus faced it). The architectural theme of the well-proportioned buildings around the Square was marked by matching horizontal banding and parapets. The bulky Masonic Lodge at the far end of Victoria Buildings was added in 1898. The water cart provided a vital service before the arrival of mains water.

Round the world yachtsman Sir Alec Rose renamed The Terminus as 'The Little Ship' in 1972. The roofline of the building has changed. Note the stone pediment surmounting the corner facing the square, which was carved by local mason Victor Saunders in the 1930s.

32. With the arrival of popular motor cars in the 1920s, three houses in Victoria Buildings were converted into a garage. The first picture was taken shortly before the devastating sea floodings of 1978 and 1979, which caused Chesil Beach Motors to retreat to higher ground on the top of Portland. Unfortunately, the steel beam supporting the upper floors was badly corroded and this section of the terrace was demolished some years later. It is awaiting future restoration.

33. The Royal Victoria Hotel helped set an imposing entrance to the Island of Portland. It was built around 1867 by influential Island leader Captain Augustus Manning of Portland Castle, on the site of an old poorhouse. The charming original Portland Station (1865) was converted to a goods station when the line to Easton was opened in 1902, three years after this picture was taken. Cab drivers await their fare in the Square as they still do a century later in somewhat different vehicles.

The Royal Victoria has now been renamed 'Masons and Mariners' and in place of the railway station – demolished in 1969 – is a floral island within the landscaped highway.

34. The original Masonic Hall of 1878 was embellished with fine carvings by E.H. Grassby, who also carved the ornate work on the adjoining arch. The latter was not the entrance to some grand house but to the Portland Gas Works! In this view in the late 1950s Aitcheson's garage served patrol over the pavement, and the Southern National Omnibus Company had a depot next door. The attractive arch is long gone and parts of this mixed frontage are now awaiting sympathetic redevelopment.

35. By the mid-1950s the compacted silt and clay bank atop Chesil Beach near Brandy Row was being eroded at an alarming rate. Had this continued Chiswell would have been left exposed to complete inundation of the sea. The ancient fisherman's cottages on the beach became derelict in the 1930s. The promenade was formed in 1959 to 1965 as part of an ambitious coast protection scheme designed by the Portland Council. The historic Cove House Inn still stands sentinel, showing that properly constructed buildings can withstand all that sea storms can throw at them. The experience here on a warm summer evening, facing the sun setting over West Bay, is priceless.

36. But in bad weather the experience can bring danger and difficulty, as this photograph of the Greek steamer *Preveza* shows. The *Preveza* ran ashore in Chesil Cove in thick fog in 1920. The photograph must have been taken as soon as the fog lifted, for smoke is still coming from the ship's funnel. Attempts to float it off failed and it finally broke in two.

37. Cove Cliff marks the end of a sharp escarpment curving around the back of Chiswell. The rough track seen here in 1900 led to West Weares, where tumbled stone blocks were collected and taken on horse-drawn carts to a masonry yard in the village. This section of the sea wall and promenade was completed in 1963. Its main function was to halt the erosion of Cove Cliff, but to residents and visitors it has opened up a great amenity.

38. The rare picture (*above*) of the West Weares in about 1875 shows the ever-slipping bank of Kimmeridge Clay descending towards the beach, lower left. The second picture (1964) shows work in progress to tackle the age-old problem of erosion and slippage in this corner of Portland. The movement was threatening not only houses and a school near the escarpment, but also the road at Priory Corner high above, right. This last section of the coast protection work was completed in 1965. It serves its engineering purpose well, and the remodelled landscape is now enjoyed by thousands of people throughout the year.

39. Countless images of this famous view have been taken since the dawn of photography in the mid-19th century. Lying in Chiswell Cove is the French schooner *Madeleine Tristan*, beached in a storm in September 1930. The crew of six was rescued and most of the cargo of grain was recovered, but the ship lay on the beach for five years. The naval oil tanks dominate the isthmus between Portland and Weymouth beyond, but behind them, the tidal waters of the Mere remain in their near-natural state. Had the Mere not been filled in for the helicopter station it would probably now have been protected as a nature reserve, for its mudflats had prolific waterfowl wildlife. The modern view on the opposite page shows how the Mere has been progressively built upon.

Underhill Junior School, locally known as 'Cliff School' (lower centre) was built on a small field at Clovens in 1913.

Victoria Gardens

40. Victoria Gardens were laid out on the sloping hillside of Little Common. A large area was levelled for tennis courts and games, and the centrepiece was an ornate bandstand, overlooked by a sunroom and pavilion. This first view was taken just after its opening in 1904; the tennis court was later moved to make room for a bowling green. The interesting background shows an industrial landscape which has totally disappeared. Behind the bandstand are the railway station yard and F.J. Barnes' stone works; while to the right was the Portland Gas Works. The Mere beyond (just visible on the extreme right) was still a natural saltwater lagoon.

Now the bandstand has gone and younger children can play safely in a new enclosed playground. The last of the 100-year-old oil tanks on the Mere are set to be removed.

41. Yet another procession, headed by a beautifully embroidered banner depicting the old and new Brackenbury churches in Fortune's Well. The young people are walking up Queen's Road past Victoria Gardens from Victoria Square.

Fortune's Well

42. After passing through the narrow streets of Fortune's Well this 1912 carnival procession is about to make the long steep climb to Tophill. The theme of this carnival was the Four Seasons, and it was organised by the Portland Men's Own Brotherhood in aid of hospitals, which were then all charity or privately funded. The small shop on the right is a saddlery, which later became a coffee shop, handy for soldiers on their way up to the Verne Citadel. The impeccable 18th-century Queen Anne house, hidden behind trees on the right, is more clearly seen in the new picture.

43. Two smiling girls in the sunshine in front of this classical Georgian chapel in Fortune's Well. This was erected in 1792 at the sole expense of Robert Carr Brackenbury, a visiting Methodist pioneer who took Portland under his wing, and who was a huge influence on Islanders. It was demolished and replaced by a manse (now a private guesthouse) after the new Methodist church was erected to its right in 1900.

44. A delightful group of youngsters pose for the camera around the turn of the 20th century. On the right is Comben's china shop, whilst the larger bay window (centre) is on the Royal Portland Arms. The second picture shows the same view about 25 years later when traction engines ruled Portland roads. The house on the left dates from the early 1700s and was where early Methodists met. Their gatherings were so rowdy that the locals nicknamed it Bedlam, a name that has stuck to that corner of Fortune's Well to this day. The 18th-century house and all the Victorian shops were demolished in the 1950s. They had suffered some bomb damage during the war but all had to give way to road widening.

45. *Top and above* A 1920s view of a long-lost street scene. Opposite the Royal Portland Arms, lofty Victorian shops and apartments contrast with the much older tiny cottage further down. With all buildings on the western side now gone, the intimacy of the old Street has vanished. On the other hand, the properties on the right now enjoy open views and sunlight.

46. *Left* A bustling Fortune's Well around 1898. The well that gave the place its name – actually a spring – can be seen under the railings (left). Shops included a chemist, grocer and boot and shoe store, and on the right can be seen the Sun Inn, one of the oldest on the island. Here on Fair Day in 1830 some 200 people were dancing inside when the floor collapsed, tipping everyone into the beer cellar below, apparently without injury!

The Sun Inn enjoyed a boom in the Second World War when it was often crowded with soldiers from a Verne Common encampment. Sadly this old pub and all the adjoining shops sustained bomb damage and were later demolished.

47. Through the 1890s the council was desperately seeking a good source for a piped water supply for Portland. In the meantime the expanding population had to get their water at the traditional places, including this spring at Fortune's Well. Some of the children are barefoot, but all seemed happy!

48. Among the Score Family's Portland businesses was this multipurpose store in Fortune's Well. The sign advertises men's and boys' clothes 'in the newest styles'; there are groceries in the window and meat hanging in the doorway. This store was later taken over by J.A. Newman who, with their branch at Easton, built up the largest grocery business on the island. After Newman's closed in the 1960s, various shops came and went until 2006 when the building was cleverly restored to its 18th-century domesticity.

49. Through the Victorian period and into the late 20th century Fortune's Well was by far the busiest shopping street on Portland. The flags (*opposite page top*) are probably for the coronation of Edward VII in August 1902, although the king had already passed through this street four months earlier. The double fronted Stanhope House is a grand and ornate building dating from 1866. The second picture (*opposite page bottom*) was taken just before the business was taken over by my grandmother Emily Morris in 1926. It was built up to be Portland's largest store, and remained in the Morris family for nearly 50 years. In 1971 (*below*), the shops here had not yet been killed off by traffic and lack of parking. From the left were Childs' hardware shop, Morris's Furnishing and Drapery emporium, Lipton's the grocer, the Post Office and the Midland bank. Apart from the Post Office, all these and the sweet shop on the right have now closed. The mantle of Portland's main shopping centre now passed to Easton.

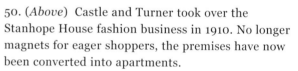

50. (*Above*) Castle and Turner took over the Stanhope House fashion business in 1910. No longer magnets for eager shoppers, the premises have now been converted into apartments.

51. (*Left*) St John's Church was built in 1839 – laterally, on the steep hillside. The sloping garden walls here give an idea of the natural gradient, which meant that even the street was cut into the slope, with retaining walls above and below it. Tradesmen's carts formed the bulk of the traffic in 1905.

52. Photographer Frederick King did not have to walk far from his Fortune's Well studio to take this picture around 1907. Children spent more time out of doors then, and nearly all wore hats. No time to hang about in the road today!

53. The hillside gets even steeper further down Fortune's Well, and early 19th century engineers had to cut through this knap to make a usable – but still steep – roadway. A prominent resident at the time was a much-respected surgeon, Doctor A.F. Meissner. He died suddenly in 1839 after 19 years' service to Portlanders, who have ever since called this place 'Meissner's Knap'. Comben's hardware shop and the butchers next door are now residences.

54. Artist Row, a narrow cul-de-sac dropping from the west side of Fortune's Well. Like many old cottages, the group on the right had roofs made of stone slat. They were demolished after suffering bomb damage in the Second World War, but for the remainder this is still a quiet retreat.

55. This part of High Street running down into Maidenwell has changed little in a hundred years, except that it is now part of the busy A354.

56. Before a public water supply was laid on in 1902 every Portland village had its wells, ponds, or as in this case, a storage cistern. Underhill had numerous natural springs emerging at various points around the hillside. These were trapped in stone storage tanks from where water could be collected by local residents. This one is in High Street opposite the Clovens junction. The stone water tank has long gone but the old wall behind it remains much as it was in 1899, and the unseen spring-water still runs.

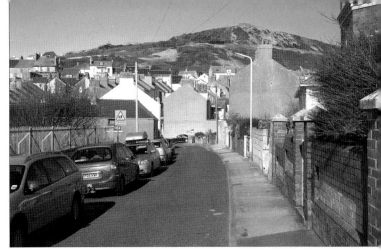

57. The 'high road and the low road' at Clovens, leading to West Weares. Children walking to the Cliff School (Underhill Junior) invariably chose to walk along the rough upper track. This road was modernised in 1963.

58. This part of High Street, facing towards Fortune's Well is dominated by comfortable bay-windowed late Victorian terraces. The refreshment shop was later a sweetshop, which closed in the 1960s.

59. The pattern of these small fields at Killicks Hill was established many hundreds of years ago. The neat dry stone walls and standing stones are of great antiquity. These upright stones marked boundaries but their unusual arrangement may point to a more mysterious purpose. The enclosures gave good produce for the Island and were clearly well maintained. Beyond, the number of boats on Chesil Beach gives an idea of the strength of the fishing industry around 1885. Remarkably some of the old stone markers can still be seen in back gardens in this now densely developed area.

60. The white building in the centre is where the children were collecting water from the cistern in the earlier photograph (number 56). These small farms caught the late morning sun, and the walls gave some shelter from the prevailing sou'westerlies. Most of the buildings in the old picture still exist and the modern view makes an interesting comparison.

61. An overview of Fortune's Well in about 1885. On the right is St. John's School, built in 1857 with the proceeds of the sale of the entire Verne Hill common to the government for the Harbour and its defences. The school was bombed in 1940, fortunately with no casualties. Between the school and St. John's Church is a field where some ten years later the imposing Ventnor Road properties were built. The white-looking road is Guernsey Street, and to the left of that is Modbury Mead which was soon to be developed with a quadrangle of terraced houses, facing High Street and Spring Gardens.

62. The steep track (left) is Old Hill, for centuries the only practical cart road between Underhill and Tophill. Its steepness was not a great problem while all the stone from the quarries was taken down over the cliffsides to the piers. However at the start of the 19th-century the need for a better route led to the New Road being built in 1810. In this picture taken a hundred years later the chimney of the Portland Steam Laundry (1900) can be seen, and in the foreground are the cowsheds of Tillycoombe Farm. The modern view shows houses on the site of the old farm, and as cattle no longer graze on the hillside, it is becoming covered with trees and shrubs.

63. The Merchants Railway of 1826 was a huge innovation in the conveyance of stone. This was the scene at the main loading point at Priory Corner around 1899. Stone blocks are being loaded onto flatbed trucks ready to be horse-drawn to the top of the incline above Castletown. On the roads, traction engines progressively took over from horses from the 1880s. The second view shows the same loading crane (centre) and the supervisor's cottage. The scene now at Priory Corner could not be more different. The old crane stood where the bank is on the left. The new deep road cutting cuts across the route of the old Merchants Railway. An old quarry derrick was restored and re-erected here in 1997 as a symbol of Portland's historic stone industry.

Priory Corner & Verne Yeates

64. The old hairpin bend was resting precariously on an old stone tip beyond the natural cliff-edge. For 20 years ground movements were monitored, and in the early 1990s the decision was made to divert the road inland. The scheme, which was completed in 1996, changed the landscape spectacularly.

65. A thunderbolt destroyed the original short-stubbed crane here in 1927. This replacement crane served until the Merchants Railway finally closed in 1939. The second photograph shows work in progress on the road scheme in October 1996, and the third the view now.

66. Processing across Verne Yeates is the funeral cortege of Rev. Canon Beazor, a revered Island leader who died in 1909. This land was quarried a century before. The same site in 1977 shows the early stages of the development of the Portland Heights Hotel. Compare this with the completed prestigious hotel today.

67. In the 1950s the landscape across north Inmosthay at the Wide Street junction, Yeates was still open and natural. In 1973, the road to Easton was diverted to the right of the 1902 castellated water reservoir. The first petrol filling station appeared on the corner in 1964, and this is the view in 2006.

68. Nothing shows the scale of 19th-century quarry engineering better than these bridges at Verne Yeates. They carried two roads and a rail tramway over a cable operated incline leading to the Merchants Railway, curving around to the lower right. The bridges are now listed Ancient Monuments and the Merchants Railway itself is a public footpath. To the right are gardens of the Tillycoombe housing estate.

69. The Verne Citadel-based Northumberland Fusiliers leaving their parade at New Ground on the 23rd of April 1898 – St. George's Day. The whole of this land was remodelled for an enormous defence scheme. The contours of vast areas were smoothed into 'glacis' to secure visibility for the Verne's big guns. The new view is also on St. George's Day, 108 years later.

70. A regiment of soldiers leaving the South Gate of Verne Citadel. The drop-bridge over the moat was later replaced by a steel girder bridge, and then a concrete one. The imposing entrance was completed in 1881.

71. Children would earn a penny or two laboriously turning the handle to raise water from a deep well, which was dug in Easton Square in 1775. This and all the other wells and pumps throughout the Island became redundant after the arrival of the piped water supply in 1902. The old well shaft is still intact under the cover seen in this path. It is some 1.5 metres in diameter and is lined with slat stone.

72. The 1907 unveiling ceremony of the stone clock tower – an attractive and practical addition to Easton Gardens.

73. Even when the band was not playing, the bandstand was a joy to look at. After dusk, the gas lamps gave a romantic aura to the gardens. A park-keeper was employed to keep everything and everybody in order.

74. (*Above & left*) Freshly planted shrubs and ornate railings adorn the new Easton Gardens. Public seats, exotic plants and mown grass were novelties at the time. The railings were taken for salvage during the Second World War, and the lovely bandstand was dismantled in the 1960s, to universal dismay.

75. (*Below*) The old well mechanism remains here in 1903, but all around the ground is being prepared for the new Easton Gardens. The Wesleyan schoolroom of 1878 was the first of several imposing buildings to be built around Easton Square. The remaining pair of cottages to its right was demolished soon after, creating space for the fine Wesleyan Chapel.

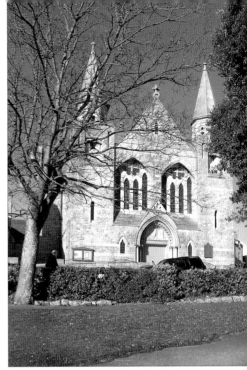

76. 1907: the scaffolding had just been removed to reveal a very photogenic place of worship, the Easton Wesleyan Chapel. Equally attractive were the young mums and their children, with their wickerwork prams, relaxing in the new gardens. Portland's population was young and vibrant at the time. Boundless energy and enthusiasm brought an unprecedented number of public buildings and works, all within a single decade.

77. This 18th-century cottage facing the Square was converted into a shop in Victorian times. It remained virtually unaltered until closing soon after this picture was taken in 1950. Almost a time capsule – its owner refused to have electricity installed – and although it is now a private house some original shop fittings are still in place today.

78. Straits in Edwardian times. The building on the left was 'Maister's School', the first on the Island, established around 1720. It had a colourful history, and was later a Reading Room, where old gossip and wisdom were exchanged. When it was demolished in 1938, the ridge-pole was found to be an old ship's mast, as sound as the day it was installed. The site is now occupied by Tophill Library, which is just visible on the extreme left and is typical 1960s architecture.

79. Jesty's at the bottom of Straits was typical of butchers in the days before electric fridges. Old Portlanders seem to have thrived on the meat hung up to the elements! What would they have made of the Oriental flavour today?

80. The plaque on the wall above the twin porches reads 'John Stevens 1734'. Most early shops were formed by installing display windows within existing cottages. The second picture was taken in 1971, some 70 years after the first, by which time an additional story had been added to two of the cottages.

Now, in the 21st century, the tiny shops of Messrs. Smith and Hooper are but memories.

81. A very quiet Easton Square in the 1920s. The shops provided the necessities of life but the depression was looming. In contrast, today Easton is now a bustling shopping centre. The only regret is that some of the ancient cottages between the shops have gone.

82. Judging by the signs in these Easton Square shops, Cadbury's was as popular hundred years ago as it is now. Attwooll's (centre) also ran a lending library.

83. Easton Street, 1899. We are now so used to the constant drone of traffic here that it is difficult to imagine how quiet things were before motor vehicles. All that could be heard were the rumble of carts and carriages, the occasional shouts of tradesmen and shrieks of children – and the sounds of nature.

84. Easton Street in 1900 displays a rich mixture of building styles and periods, the reason for its Conservation Area status. Shops have come and gone through the generations. In the distance on the right, at Grove Corner, can be seen a 'township' of temporary houses for contractors working on the second stage of the Breakwaters.

85. Until the early 19th century, simple thatched or stone-roofed cottages like this one in Easton Street were to be found in all the Portland villages. Compare and contrast!

86. The Portland Steam Laundry was founded at Underhill in 1900. Clothes were collected and delivered in this cart, which is stopped at a 'filling station' in Easton Lane. The ornate cast-iron trough still exists (in a private garden). Beyond (left) is the range of buildings of the Crown Farm, which suffered severe bomb damage in the Second World War. The modern buildings on their site blend in well with the street scene.

87. Further up Easton Lane was the Saw Mill Tavern, which took its name from the stone cutting mills behind it. Here now is Chesil Beach Motors, which moved from Chiswell after 1980.

88. Not as grand as its London namesake (the home of the Duke of Wellington), but Apsley House in Reforne is dated 1815, the year of Wellington's victory at the Battle of Waterloo. Next door is Fancy's Garage, a fondly remembered family business. It was already well established here in 1950 and finally closed some 35 years later.

89. Reforne was once a separate hamlet from Easton, and its origins are as ancient as any on Portland. As elsewhere some of the Victorian houses were built on centuries-old foundations.

90. Another view of Apsley House, its tiny neighbouring cottage contrasting with the taller mid Victorian houses.

91. The driver of this 1920s open top tourer may have popped into the George Inn for a quick one. This inn is steeped in history, and it has retained its old character. The Court Leet made important decisions there, as did Portland's smugglers, in dimly-lit rooms.

92. The rare snow-bound winter of 1962/63 nearly stopped Portland in its tracks for 3 months. It did stop work on the open-air Portcrete works at Wide Street, so a huge shed was later built to cover it. Here were made the huge precast units for London's 1960s icon, the Centre Point skyscraper. It is now a fibreglass works.

The Grove

93. Armed warders pose by the original (1848) gateway to the Grove convict prison. This photograph sold by the hundreds to Edwardian visitors. The prison closed after the Great War, and in 1921 it became a Borstal Institution. It is now a Young Offenders Institution. The central gateway remains unchanged, but a modern administration block replaces the Victorian houses.

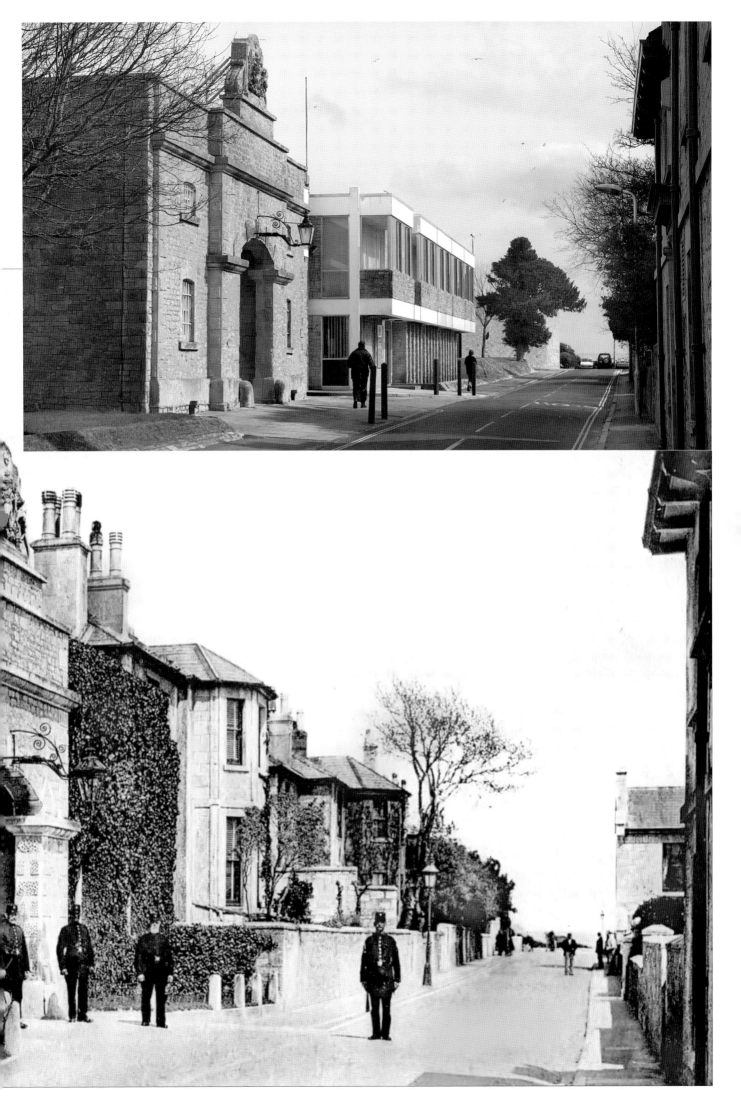

94. The clifftop jail was built in 1848 to house prisoners quarrying stone for the Breakwaters. This is Rodney House, one of five huge stone accommodation blocks, as rebuilt 1896-1908. Four Borstal boys were killed when it was bombed on the 15th August 1940. The raid also destroyed the two cottages beyond the wall and a chapel. The unusual obelisk is a Victorian ventilation shaft, now an Ancient Monument. The cliff road is a public footpath.

95. The photographer got down to child's eye level to capture these convicts filling a water tanker in about 1905. The warders' houses in Grove Road (right) were known as The Alma; they were built in 1854, the year of the Crimean battle of that name.

96. The Grove was developed from almost nothing when work started on the Breakwater, Verne Citadel and convict prison in the 1850s. However, there is some evidence of much older habitation in this part of Portland. These simple stone cottages in Grove Road remain externally much as they were in the 1890s, apart from the loss of the railings and ivy.

97. One of Portland's spectacular secrets is hardly seen by any visitors today. This impressive sports stadium at The Grove took four years to create from an old convict quarry. It was completed in time for these Borstal Games in 1936. In 2006 the stadium is dormant, awaiting new access and facilities. Like so many parts of Portland, the site has enormous potential.

Wakeham & Church Ope

98. The incredibly wide road characterises Wakeham, one of Portland's oldest hamlets. The horse and cart was probably more at ease on the rough road surface than the motorcycle parked on the left (circa 1926).

99. Another doomed legacy from Portland Past. In the centre is the old thatched cottage in Wakeham of Joe Bowring, one of Portland's last shepherds. He was devastated when it burnt down in 1929.

100. (*Above*) At one time 19th-century Portland had more inns and pubs per head of population than most places. This is surprising as most Islanders were staunchly Methodist, and drink was (theoretically) frowned upon. Note the caged songbird to the left of the cottage door. This is the Queen of the Valley, now replaced by the equally exotically named Alessandria Hotel.

101. Most of Wakeham's old cottages have changed little in a hundred years. Robust stone porches kept the draught out of many of the smaller cottages.

102. Parking was not a problem in 1928 especially in wide Wakeham, although the traction engines left the unsurfaced roads in a terrible state.

103. The ancient hamlet of Wakeham originally centred on the top of the dell leading down to Church Ope Cove. These well-weathered old cottages date from the early 17th century, although parts of some buildings are probably centuries older. The cottage on the right is now Portland Museum, which is also shown on the opposite page.

104. We are fortunate that Portland lover and benefactor Dr Marie Stopes saw beauty in the Island's traditional cottages. She had this one restored and turned into the picturesque Portland Museum in 1930, seen here from the lane leading down to Church Ope Cove.

105. Rufus Castle has stood on its pinnacle of rock high above Church Ope Cove for at least 600 years. Its original Norman-style arch was replaced by a wider one in the early 19th century. Unfortunately, this seaward feature collapsed in 1989 and restoration is awaited. In the foreground are the remains of the Island's first known church, the 13th century St. Andrew's. Its historic graveyard suffered some Second World War bomb damage; the little doorway arch was broken but now rests in Portland Museum.

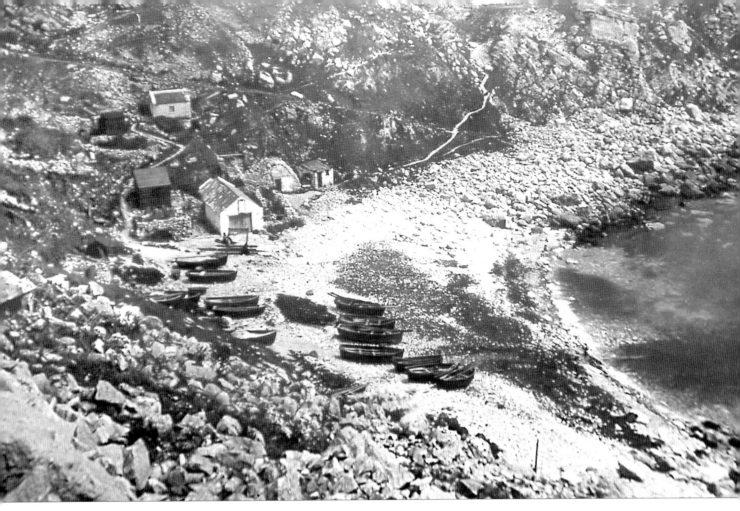

106. Church Ope Cove (here in about 1880) played a big part in Portland's history. This was the scene of French raids in the 13th century, the shipping of stone from short piers, and fishing. The stone building on the beach was originally a Revenue boathouse for anti-smuggling operations – a lost cause here! The now tranquil cove is less recessed than it used to be, due to stone waste tipped over the cliffs near Southwell in the early 20th century being washed along the coast.

Weston

107. Butcher William Morris (my great-grandfather) doing his rounds in Gypsy Lane, Weston in 1898. Of the pair of thatched cottages just visible on the left, one went the way of many of Portland's 17th-century houses, but the other has been lovingly restored. Local folklore says that here was the first house on Portland to have glass windows – the old Lugger Inn.

108. Not some little town in the Australian Outback but a barren looking Weston in 1904. On the cart is Mr Cox, shopkeeper of Easton, delivering his goods.

109. The Royal Exchange Inn, Weston Road, was named after the magnificent London building for which Portland supplied the stone. Here in 1897 staff, customers and local children gather for a picture. The tall gentleman with one leg shorter than the other was a character known as 'Admiral Hardy'. A flat roofed extension was created later, over the pavement.

110. A tiny corner shop, created in the front room of Mrs Elliott's house at Weston, served the village with its day-to-day needs. Behind it is number 72, a rare surviving wing of a very substantial Tudor house built in the 1500s.

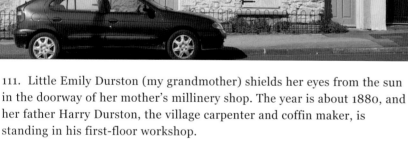

111. Little Emily Durston (my grandmother) shields her eyes from the sun in the doorway of her mother's millinery shop. The year is about 1880, and her father Harry Durston, the village carpenter and coffin maker, is standing in his first-floor workshop.

112. On the east side of Weston Road, this shop has been through various phases. Here in 1921, hidden slightly behind the flags decorating a children's fête, it is a ladies and gents outfitter, and it was later the village post office. In the early 21st century it is a popular specialist bistro restaurant.

113. Weston Pond circa 1898. All Tophill's villages had one or two ponds in addition to wells. They were fed by natural watercourses, which generally ran through ancient stone culverts. The ponds served their purposes well through countless centuries, but they were all filled in after the arrival of a piped water supply in 1902. The basic arrangement of houses in the area remains much the same, but the fine cast iron lamp standard reflected in the pond has long gone.

114. Boys rest on the old wall by Weston Pond in 1899. We do not know its age, but the area was inhabited in Roman times. Away to the right is the road to Southwell, and centre is the Prince Alfred Inn – after the royal prince who came to Portland several times during the building of the Breakwaters. A single gas lamp surmounted a large stone on the green, which also contained a post box.

115. These cavernous late 19th-century barns and stables at Weston Street housed trucks, horses and carts for the stone industry. When the site was redeveloped in 1984, large stone arches on the front (not visible in this pair of photographs) were recreated in the new houses.

116. For more than a thousand years farming was a vital part of the Portland economy. Right up to the end of the 19th century farmland stretched from coast to coast, and from Portland Bill to north of Easton. This is the North Mill, one of two windmills in Droop Field. Grain from the Tophill fields was taken here for grinding.

117. Until 1991, South or Angel Mill remained almost surrounded by fields. It took but a few weeks for the pasture to its left to be quarried away, but the fields beyond towards Weston remain; a vital vestige of Portland's agrarian landscape. The 400-year-old windmills last turned in the 1890s. They are extremely rare, and are surely worthy of restoration.

Southwell

118. (*Above & left*) The road over the hill from Weston rejoiced in the name 'Slobs'. It was renamed 'Avalanche Road' after the terrible collision between the ships *Avalanche* and *Forest* off this coast in 1877 with the loss of 108 lives. Within only two years of the disaster the Avalanche Memorial Church, St. Andrews, was completed.

119. (*Below*) A rare glimpse of Southwell's pond in its twilight years. From here, its spring water ran in a tiny stream down through the village (nicknamed 'Duck Town') and over the cliff at Freshwater Bay. The site is now a children's playground – but it was always thus.

120. Despite its poor quality, this rare photograph shows the section of the road to the Bill known as High Street, but in 1905 it was still little more than a cattle drove. It gave access to the fields and the cliffs but little else, and tourists rarely ventured this far south.

121. It seems that only the early photographers appreciated the picturesque 17th-century cottages, which abounded on Portland – so many were destroyed through neglect or decree. This once charming pair faced the road to the Bill in Southwell Square. Remarkably a finely cut stone mullioned window still survives in what is now a garden wall.

122. A scattering of street lamps appeared in the Portland villages after the Portland gas works was built in 1865. This is Southwell Square around the turn of the 20th century. To the left can be seen the pair of thatched cottages in the previous photographs.

123. Southwell folk loved to go to their homely little Methodist Chapel, seen here in about 1925. The villagers built this for themselves in 1836. Earlier, Methodist pioneer Charles Wesley wrote in his diary: – '1746: June 9th – . . . at Southwell, the farthest village, I expounded the Song of Simeon. Some very old men attended. I distributed a few books among them . . . My mouth and their hearts were opened. The rocks were broken in pieces, and melted into tears on every side.'

The chapel closed in 1996 and is now a private house.

124. The intriguingly-named Eight King's Inn has long been a focal point of Southwell. A 17th-century – or earlier – thatched cottage stands alongside the road to the Bill.

125. In its tranquil setting, with rolling fields on three sides, Dorset's southernmost village was a rural idyll. This farmer is returning his cattle to his Southwell farmyard down the stony Sweet Hill Road. This road was made up in 1950 to access the huge Admiralty research establishment on Barrow Hill, which is now Southwell Business Park.

126. Not so old, but now a different world. Here in 1971 are still the ancient fields of Bown Hill (foreground), Sweet Hill (upper left) and Barrow Hill (upper right) where stands the great Admiralty research establishment. The strip fields and lynchets were a rare survival from pre-mediaeval times. Over 30 years this pastoral landscape was changed into a vast housing estate, completed in 2005.

127. Reap Lane in 1971, and 35 years later. The boundary walls of enormous stone blocks are ancient features of this part of Portland. The fields here have produced evidence of Iron Age, Roman and mediaeval occupation.

The Admiralty complex on the skyline is now the Southwell Business Park.

128. The road to Southwell near Cheyne passes old walled enclosures, which were a part of the great Coombe Field. Each sector of land had its own fascinating place-name. The last of these ancient fields were dug away for quarrying in 2006.

The large structure (centre) in the photograph below is the former Perryfield Stone Works. Currently a marine engineering factory, it is due to be replaced by a group of attractive houses.

Portland Bill

129. The first Portland Bill lighthouses were built in 1716, and had a bright if not always successful history. They operated as a pair, the Higher Light being high on Branscombe Hill, a superb vantage point for a wide sweep of the English Channel. Both the Higher and Lower lighthouses were rebuilt in 1867. These men are removing the working equipment from the old Higher Lighthouse after it was superseded by the new lighthouse in 1906. This is now a lovely private residence and holiday apartments.

130. The old Lower Lighthouse was rebuilt in 1867 near the site of the original tower of 1716. The whole complex — tower, keepers' cottages and garden walls – were whitewashed to be visible from the sea. These mid-Victorian lights had a life of only 40 years, being rapidly overtaken by newer technology. This is now an important ornithology and bird study centre.

131. Builders Wakeham Bros did not have to go far for the stone for the new Portland Bill lighthouse. The timber scaffolding creaked and swayed in the wind, but the tower was successfully completed, and was first lit in 1906. The foundations are over 2 metres deep in the bedrock.

The old Lower Light can be seen on the right.

132. The precision lamp and a lens assembly of the new lighthouse weighed several tons. Although it was delivered in kit form raising it up the 43m tower in 1905 using only hand-powered mechanisms was a highly skilled feat. Illumination was initially by an oil lamp, rotated by clockwork, but everything was electrified in 1952.

133. Rarely can an old picture be so accurately dated; this was noon on the 27th September 1893. The John Pearce Stone Company had opened this quarry in the common lands at Portland Bill. Although remote, the advantage was a shallow overburden (which incidentally comprised the now famous raised beach). From here, horses drew trucks on a short tramway to the cliff edge, from where the stone was loaded into barges. A precarious fair-weather operation, but sometimes 100 tons a day were shipped off.

134. After a proper road to the Bill was laid in 1922, and with the coming of charabancs in the 1930s, tourists started to flock to Portland Bill. Seen here from the top of the lighthouse are the teahouses and café, and the shallow cutting of the old stone tramway on which a single horse drew a four-wheeled truck from the little quarry to the cliffside crane. The second view is from the lighthouse in its centenary year. The popular Lobster Pot restaurant has been rebuilt, but the biggest change is in the distant fields, where hundreds of recreational huts enable visitors and residents alike to spend lazy days in the bracing air and sun on this rugged coast. *Photo by S. Morris by courtesy of the Corporation of Trinity House.*

The Railway

135. Finally a few glimpses of a much-missed phase in Portland's history – the railway. The first passengers arrived at Easton Station in September 1902. This neat stone building was just a minute's walk from the centre of Easton. All this has now vanished in this treed and landscaped area, where now stands the Lady Mead Hall elderly persons residence.

136. A sequence of views of the railway cutting under Yeolands Bridge high above Church Ope Cove. The second picture is the author sketching the scene in the late 1950s. In the third view the arch has long been demolished, trees have grown up, and the cliff is a lure for climbers (right).

137. Portland's railway, climbing through the East Weares towards Easton was one of the most scenic in the country. Had it not closed to passengers in 1952 it would have been a jewel in the local tourist scene. To the right is Little Beach, which unlike Church Ope Cove is now more deeply recessed than in the past.

138. The railway line below Yeoland Cliffs. In the second photograph, taken in the 1920s, the field on the left has been quarried. In the third photograph a group of climbers prepare to ascend the Cliffs. This part of the old railway route is now a spectacular walk: Portland is now part of the South-West Coastal Path, one of England's nationally designated trails.

139. As can be seen by the terrain, this line was very difficult and costly to construct, one reason why it failed to pay its way. The promontory in the distance is Godnor Point.

140. The end of the line for Portland's railway finally came in 1971 when the track was removed. The grassland here on the Chesil causeway has been restored to common, but the scene behind is vastly different; it is now evolving as the Weymouth & Portland National Sailing Academy.

141. We are now back where we started, by Ferry Bridge. This railway viaduct of 1902 replaced the original bridge built in 1864. It was demolished in 1971, and recreation is now the theme around the Smallmouth area.

PORTRAITS, MINIATURES, ENLARGEMENTS

FRED. W. GEORGE
THE REGENT STUDIOS

63 FORTUNE'S WELL
PORTLAND.

THE FAVOUR OF YOUR
RECOMMENDATION
WILL BE ESTEEMED.

DAY & EVENING
STUDIOS.

PORTRAITS
AND
Landscape
PHOTOGRAPHERS
Billinghurst &

Lowe
WEYM
Fortu
PORT
AND
JER

NEGATIVES KEPT COPIES CAN ALWAYS BE OBTAINED.

Enlargements made and finished in Oil Water or Crayons.

THE REGENT
STUDIOS

144 FORTUNE'S WELL

PORTLAND

Fred. W. George

DAY & EVENING
STUDIOS.

DUPLICATES CAN BE HAD AT ANY
TIME AT REDUCED RATES.

NEGATIVES PRESERVED.